A FIRST LOOK AT AMERICA'S PRESIDENTS

FRANKLIN D. ROOSEVELT

The 32nd President

by Josh Gregory

Consultant: Meena Bose
Director, Peter S. Kalikow Center for the Study of the American Presidency
Peter S. Kalikow Chair in Presidential Studies
Professor, Political Science
Hofstra University
Hempstead, New York

BEARPORT
PUBLISHING

New York, New York

Credits

Cover, © Bettmann/Corbis/AP Images; 4, © Bettmann/Corbis/AP Images; 5T, © Pictorial Press Ltd/Alamy; 5B, © Associated Press; 6, © Liz Van Steenburgh/Shutterstock; 7L, © Everett Collection Inc/Alamy; 7R, © Everett Collection Inc/Alamy; 8, Courtesy of the U.S. National Archives and Records Administration; 9, © Everett Collection Inc/Alamy; 10, Courtesy of the Library of Congress; 11, Courtesy of the Library of Congress; 12, Courtesy of the Library of Congress; 13T, Courtesy of the Library of Congress; 13B, Courtesy of the Library of Congress; 14, Courtesy of the U.S. National Archives and Records Administration; 15, © Keith Tarrier/Shutterstock; 16, © Bettmann/Corbis; 17T, © Bettmann/Corbis/AP Images; 17B, © peresanz/Shutterstock; 18, Courtesy of the Library of Congress; 19T, © Richard Cavalleri/Shutterstock; 19B, © Pete Spiro/Shutterstock; 20T, Courtesy of the U.S. National Archives and Records Administration; 20B, © Liz Van Steenburgh/Shutterstock; 21, © Keith Tarrier/Shutterstock; 22, © Wendy Kaveney Photography/Shutterstock; 23T, Courtesy of the Library of Congress; 23B, © B. Speckart/Shutterstock.

Publisher: Kenn Goin
Editor: Joyce Tavolacci
Creative Director: Spencer Brinker
Design: The Design Lab
Photo Researcher: Jennifer Zeiger

Special thanks to fifth-grader Lucy Barr and second-grader Brian Barr for their help in reviewing this book.

Library of Congress Cataloging-in-Publication Data

Gregory, Josh.
  Franklin D. Roosevelt : the 32nd president / by Josh Gregory.
      pages cm. — (A first look at America's presidents)
  Includes bibliographical references and index.
  ISBN 978-1-62724-555-5 (library binding) — ISBN 1-62724-555-3 (library binding)
  1. Roosevelt, Franklin D. (Franklin Delano), 1882-1945. 2. Presidents—United States—Biography—Juvenile literature.
I. Title.
  E807.G74 2015
  973.917092—dc23
  [B]
                                        2014029075

For more information, write to Bearport Publishing Company, Inc., 45 West 21st Street, Suite 3B,
New York, New York 10010. Printed in the United States of America.

10 9 8 7 6 5 4 3 2 1

CONTENTS

A Leader in Tough Times

As president, Franklin D. Roosevelt faced tough times. Many Americans were out of work. They had little money to buy food. Also, countries around the world were at war.

In the 1930s, hungry people waited in long lines for free food.

Franklin D. Roosevelt was the 32nd president. He served from 1933 to 1945.

Franklin D. Roosevelt was often called FDR for short.

Roosevelt was president during World War II (1939–1945).

5

Starting Out in New York

Franklin D. Roosevelt was born in Hyde Park, New York, in 1882. His family was very wealthy. Yet they helped those who had less. As Franklin grew older, he wanted to help people by serving in government. When he was 28, he was **elected** to the New York **State Senate**.

Franklin grew up in this large house in Hyde Park.

Franklin was an only child.

Other people in Franklin's family also served in government. His cousin, Theodore Roosevelt, became president in 1901.

Theodore Roosevelt

A Sudden Setback

Franklin D. Roosevelt had to stop doing his government work in 1921. That year, he got a terrible illness called polio. It **paralyzed** his legs. Roosevelt tried hard, but he was never able to walk again.

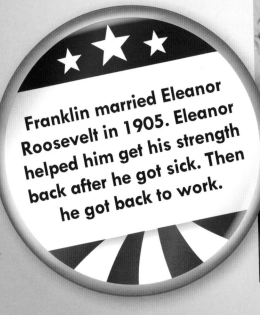

Franklin married Eleanor Roosevelt in 1905. Eleanor helped him get his strength back after he got sick. Then he got back to work.

Franklin and Eleanor Roosevelt sit with their first two children. During their marriage, they had six children together.

Roosevelt used leg braces and special platforms, like this one, to help him stand up.

9

Hard Times for America

In 1929, Roosevelt became **governor** of New York. That same year, hard times hit the country. Many businesses failed. Millions of people lost their jobs. They were left without money, food, or places to live. This time was known as the **Great Depression**.

The Great Depression began in 1929.

Many people in cities could not find work during the Great Depression.

Some people traveled around the country looking for work on farms. They often lived in simple tents or in their cars.

A New Deal

Roosevelt wanted to help end the Depression. In 1932, he ran for president and won. He then put together a plan called the New Deal. It created new jobs. Slowly, the country began to recover.

Eleanor Roosevelt spoke to people about Franklin's work as president.

Work Pays America!

PROSPERITY

WORKS PROGRESS ADMINISTRATION

People built bridges, roads, and even schools as part of the New Deal.

Posters like this one helped people learn about Roosevelt's plan for creating jobs.

13

The World at War

Soon, Roosevelt faced another huge problem. In 1939, World War II began in Europe. Then it spread to other places. In 1941, Japan attacked the United States. Roosevelt decided to fight back. The United States joined the war.

During the Depression, Roosevelt started giving talks about his plans on the radio. He kept giving the talks during the war.

Roosevelt tried to make his radio talks friendly and helpful. They were known as Fireside Chats.

Japan attacked the U.S.
Navy at Pearl Harbor
in Hawaii in 1941.

Peace at Last

Roosevelt met with the leaders of other countries. Together, they planned ways to win the war and bring about peace. Sadly, Roosevelt died in 1945 before the war was over. Four months later, the United States helped end the war.

Roosevelt worked closely with Winston Churchill (right) of Great Britain.

American soldiers in Paris, France

World War II was the worst war in history. About 17 million soldiers died.

A cemetery in France where many World War II soldiers are buried

Remembering Roosevelt

Millions of Americans felt a deep loss when Roosevelt died. The world had lost a strong, bold leader. Today, we remember Franklin D. Roosevelt as a great president who steered the country through hard times and war.

Roosevelt is the only president elected four times. Today, presidents can be elected only twice.

Crowds of Americans came to see Roosevelt's coffin carried through the streets.

There is a memorial for Roosevelt in Washington, D.C.

THEY (WHO) SEEK TO ESTABLISH SYSTEMS OF GOVERNMENT BASED ON THE REGIMENTATION OF ALL HUMAN BEINGS BY A HANDFUL OF INDIVIDUAL RULERS... CALL THIS A NEW ORDER. IT IS NOT NEW AND IT IS NOT ORDER.

Roosevelt's face appears on the front of the dime.

TIMELINE

Here are some major events from Franklin D. Roosevelt's life.

1882
Franklin D. Roosevelt is born in Hyde Park, New York.

1905
Franklin and Eleanor Roosevelt marry.

 1880 **1890** **1900** **1910**

1900
When Roosevelt is 18 years old, his father, James Roosevelt, dies.

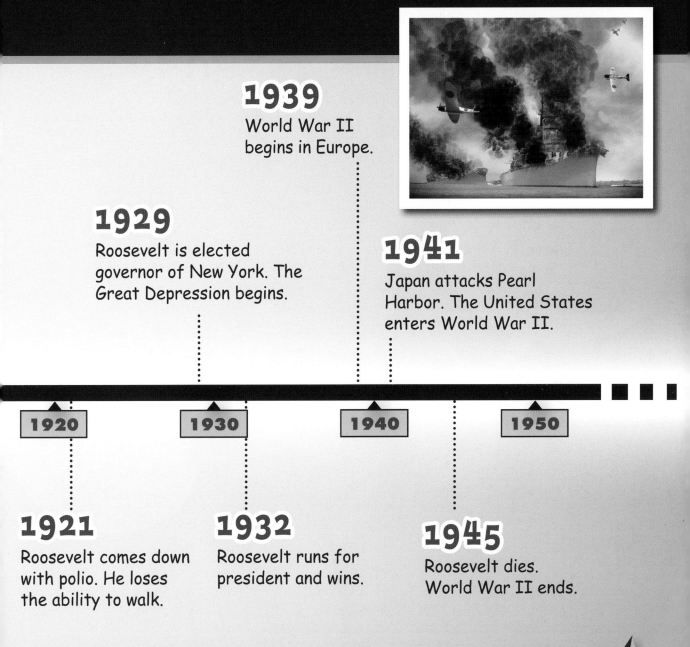

1939
World War II
begins in Europe.

1929
Roosevelt is elected
governor of New York. The
Great Depression begins.

1941
Japan attacks Pearl
Harbor. The United States
enters World War II.

| 1920 | 1930 | 1940 | 1950 |

1921
Roosevelt comes down
with polio. He loses
the ability to walk.

1932
Roosevelt runs for
president and wins.

1945
Roosevelt dies.
World War II ends.

"I pledge you, I pledge myself, to a new deal for the American people."

Roosevelt started collecting stamps at age eight. During his lifetime, he collected more than one million stamps.

"The only thing we have to fear is fear itself."

Eleanor Roosevelt was the niece of President Theodore Roosevelt.

elected (i-LEKT-id) chosen by vote

governor (GUHV-urn-ur) the head of a state

Great Depression (GRAYT di-PRESH-uhn) a period from 1929 to the 1930s when many people lost their jobs and had little money

paralyzed (PAR-uh-lyezd) made unable to move or feel a part of the body

state senate (STAYT SEN-uht) a group of people who make laws within a state

Index

Read More

Edison, Erin. *Franklin D. Roosevelt (Presidential Biographies).* North Mankato, MN: Capstone (2013).

Wood, Douglas. *Franklin and Winston: A Christmas That Changed the World.* Cambridge, MA: Candlewick (2011).

Learn More Online

To learn more about Franklin D. Roosevelt, visit
www.bearportpublishing.com/AmericasPresidents

About the Author:
Josh Gregory writes and edits books for kids. He lives in Chicago, Illinois.